GRAPHIC HISTORY

THE CURSE OF
KING TUT'S
TOMB

by Michael Burgan
illustrated by Barbara Schulz

Consultant:
Carolyn Graves Brown
Curator, Egypt Centre, University of Wales Swansea
Swansea, Wales

Capstone
press

Mankato, Minnesota

Graphic Library is published by Capstone Press,
151 Good Counsel Drive, P.O. Box 669, Mankato, Minnesota 56002.
www.capstonepub.com

 Books published by Capstone Press are manufactured with paper
containing at least 10 percent post-consumer waste.

Library of Congress Cataloging-in-Publication Data
Burgan, Michael.
  The curse of King Tut's tomb / by Michael Burgan; illustrated by Barbara Schulz.
  p. cm.—(Graphic library. Graphic history)
  Includes bibliographical references and index.
  ISBN-13: 978-0-7368-3833-7 (hardcover) ISBN-13: 978-0-7368-5244-9 (softcover pbk.)
  ISBN-10: 0-7368-3833-3 (hardcover)   ISBN-10: 0-7368-5244-1 (softcover pbk.)
  1. Tutankhamen, King of Egypt—Tomb—Juvenile literature. 2. Blessing and cursing—
  Egypt—Juvenile literature. I. Barbara Schulz, ill. II. Title. III. Series.
DT87.5.B83 2005
932'.014—dc22   2004020452

Summary: Follows the discovery and excavation of King Tutankhamen's tomb and the myth
of the curse that afflicted those involved in the tomb's exploration.

Editor's note: Direct quotations from primary sources are indicated by a yellow background.
Direct quotations appear on the following pages:
Pages 9, 11, 14, from *The Tomb of Tut.ankh.Amen, Discovered by the Late Earl of Carnarvon
and Howard Carter* by Howard Carter and A. C. Mace (London: Cassell and Company,
Ltd., 1923).
Page 21, from "Effects of Digestive Disfunction" by Dr. Skye Weintraub
(http://www.femcentre.com/digestive1.pdf).
Page 22, from *The Complete Tutankhamun: The King, the Tomb, the Royal Treasure*
by Nicholas Reeves (New York: Thames and Hudson, 1990).

Art Directors
Jason Knudson
Heather Kindseth

Storyboard Artists
Sandra D'Antonio
Jason Knudson

Colorist
Ben Hunzeker

Editor
Amanda Doering

Acknowledgment
Capstone Press thanks Philip Charles
Crawford, Library Director, Essex High
School, Essex, Vermont, and columnist
for *Knowledge Quest*, for his assistance
in the preparation of this book.

Printed in the United States of America in Stevens Point, Wisconsin.
112011
006465R

TABLE OF CONTENTS

Chapter 1

The Mummy's Curse is Born

More than 5,000 years ago, a rich and powerful kingdom developed along the Nile River in Egypt. Today, people call the kings of Egypt pharaohs.

At first, ancient Egyptians built huge pyramids in which they buried their kings. Later, they buried their kings in underground tombs.

Ancient Egyptians believed their kings' spirits lived on after death. The tombs protected the kings' spirits and held everything they would need in the afterworld.

Egyptians mummified the dead so their spirits could return to their bodies. Some of the king's organs were removed and placed in jars that were left in the tomb.

Egyptian priests cast spells over the dead king's body. They placed precious stones or pieces of metal in the strips of cloth wound around the body. Writings on the wall warned grave robbers not to disturb the tomb.

May these spells and this magical stone protect your spirit forever. May the great god judge anyone who steals from this tomb.

What do you think is inside? Gold? Jewels?

Probably just dust from old bones. He's been dead for more than 3,000 years.

I've heard mummies are cursed. We should leave the dead alone.

The idea of a mummy's curse spread. Writers created stories about people who died horrible deaths after disturbing mummies. These stories did not stop archaeologists from exploring the tombs.

One of these scientists was England's Howard Carter. During the early 1900s, he worked in Egypt's Valley of the Kings for Lord Carnarvon. Lord Carnarvon was deeply interested in Egyptian artifacts.

In the Valley of the Kings, the kings' tombs were deep underground. By 1909, many people believed the major tombs there had been found. Carter disagreed. He wanted to find the tomb of Tutankhamen, known as King Tut. Tutankhamen ruled Egypt more than 3,000 years ago.

It's been years, Carter. Lord Carnarvon's money is running out. We can't keep digging much longer.

Something will turn up. I think Tut's tomb is nearby.

We've found something!

It looks like the entrance to a tomb.

Chapter 2

An Amazing Discovery

Three weeks later, Carter and his men had cleared out the passageway to a sealed doorway. Beyond this door, another sealed doorway stood outside King Tut's tomb. Lord Carnarvon waited anxiously for the plaster to be removed.

This doorway has been opened and sealed before. Grave robbers must have found it centuries ago.

There may be nothing left inside.

Carter and his crew began exploring the tomb and its treasures. They numbered each item they found. It would take Carter years to examine everything in the tomb's many rooms.

What is it?

It's a royal robe, covered with beads and tiny pieces of gold.

And look at these couches. They're made of gold!

Around this time, a mosquito bit Lord Carnarvon's face.

Soon after, while he was shaving...

First the mosquito bite and now this. What a nasty mess this is going to be.

The cut on Lord Carnarvon's mosquito bite led to blood poisoning. He recovered, but he soon became sick again.

I'm afraid you have pneumonia. You need rest.

THE CURSE AT WORK

Marie Corelli, a famous New York author, heard about Carnarvon's poor health. It reminded her of something she had read in an old book about ancient Egypt.

It says here there was an inscription outside Tut's tomb that read, "Death shall come on swift wings to him who touches the tomb of the pharaoh."

Did the mosquito bite make Lord Carnarvon so sick, or could it be a mummy's curse?

CURSE OR MYTH?

Carter and Callender both lived for more than a decade after opening Tut's coffin.

You've made history, Carter. No one has ever found anything like Tut's tomb. And you even escaped that silly curse.

I told you the talk of a curse was rubbish. We knew that tomb better than anyone. If there had been a written curse, we'd have seen it.

Even though the curse hadn't affected Carter or Callender, some people still believed it was real. Herbert Winlock, an expert on ancient Egypt, set out to prove the believers wrong.

	NUMBER OF PEOPLE ATTENDING	NUMBER OF PEOPLE WHO DIED WITHIN 10 YEARS
OPENING OF BURIAL CHAMBER	26	6
UNWRAPPING OF MUMMY	10	0

The numbers don't lie, gentlemen. The people who died were mostly older people, or people already in poor health. The only curse at work is the curse that all people eventually die. Life killed these poor souls, not a mummy's curse.

Reports of strange events related to Tut's tomb stopped. But every so often, a new story was added to the curse's legend.

In 1966, Mohammed Ibrahim, Egypt's director of antiquities, dreamed he would face great danger if Tut's artifacts left Egypt.

No! Noooooo!

Almost 100 years after Tut's discovery, people are still fascinated and frightened by the idea of a mummy's curse. Movies and books about mummies still scare audiences even today. The legend of Tut's curse lives on.

AAAAAAAH!

Do you think Tut's tomb was cursed?

Of course not. Scientists say people who entered Tut's tomb were no more likely to die early than those who hadn't been near the tomb.

But would you spend a night in a mummy's tomb?

Are you kidding? Never!

- Many deaths of people connected with King Tut's tomb were odd and mysterious. It's not surprising that these unexplained deaths were mistaken as the result of a curse. One example is the death of Richard Bethell, Howard Carter's personal secretary. Bethell's father, Lord Westbury, killed himself after hearing of his son's death. The car carrying Lord Westbury's body to the cemetery struck and killed an eight-year-old boy.

- King Tut was buried in a tomb meant for someone else. Other ancient Egyptians' names appear on many of the artifacts left in Tut's tomb. Even one of the coffins he is buried in has someone else's name on it.

- Grave robbers probably broke into Tut's tomb shortly after he died. They were caught before much damage was done. Priests reburied the entrance to Tut's tomb, and it stayed buried until Carter found it in 1922.

- Howard Carter was more concerned about getting the treasures from Tut's tomb than in preserving the body. Carter cut Tut's body in three pieces. Today, Tut's body lies in his original burial place. It is carefully protected by the Egyptian government.

Howard Carter found the mummies of two of King Tut's children in the king's tomb. Scientists think both children were female.

Scientists believe that some people who entered Tut's tomb died because of mold or fungus that grew in the tomb. Many kinds of harmful bacteria have been found in Tut's tomb.

Some scientists believe King Tut was murdered. He was only 18 or 19 when he died. X-rays of Tut's skull show that he suffered a blow to the back of his head. He was buried very quickly. The next ruler tried to erase history by removing all records of Tut from official documents.

GLOSSARY

archaeologist (ar-kee-OL-uh-jist)—a scientist who studies the past by looking at old buildings and objects

artifact (AR-tih-fakt)—an object made by humans that was used in the past; tools and weapons are artifacts.

contempt (kuhn-TEMPT)—total lack of respect

excavation (ek-skuh-VAY-shuhn)—a search for ancient remains buried in the ground

exhibit (eg-ZIB-it)—a public display of works of art or historical objects

pneumonia (noo-MOH-nyuh)—a serious disease that makes breathing very difficult

spirit (SPIHR-it)—the part of a person thought to control thoughts and feelings; ancient Egyptians believed the spirit left the body after death and traveled to the afterworld.

INTERNET SITES

FactHound offers a safe, fun way to find Internet sites related to this book. All of the sites on FactHound have been researched by our staff.

Here's how:

1. *Visit www.facthound.com*
2. Type in this special code **0736838333** for age-appropriate sites. Or enter a search word related to this book for a more general search.
3. Click on the **Fetch It** button.

FactHound will fetch the best sites for you!